Scripture Confessions
for Kids

by
Harrison House

Harrison House
Tulsa, Oklahoma 74153

All Scripture quotations are taken from the
King James Version of the Bible.

13 12 11 10   20 19 18 17 16

Scripture Confessions for Kids
ISBN 13: 978-1-57794-037-1
ISBN 10: 1-57794-037-7
(formerly ISBN 0-89274-322-0)
Copyright © 1984, 2003 by Harrison House

Illustrations by Lisa Browning

Published by Harrison House, Inc.
P.O. Box 35035
Tulsa, Oklahoma 74153

God is the strength of
my life. I can do anything
with Jesus in me.

(Psalm 27:1; Philippians 4:13.)

I love others
because You
first loved me.

(Ephesians 5:2.)

I am taught of the Lord,
and His peace
belongs to me.

(Isaiah 54:13.)

I am an overcomer!
Your Word makes me
a winner all the time.

(2 Corinthians 2:14.)

Jesus is my light.
I will let my light shine
all the time so everyone
can see Jesus in me.

(John 1:4; Matthew 5:16.)

Thank You for forgiving
me of everything bad
I've ever done and for
taking sickness away
from my life so I can
be well and praise You.

(Psalm 103:2,3.)

I will give thanks and
sing praises to the
Lord all the time.

(Psalm 92:1.)

I will always respect
and obey my father and
mother so my life will
be long and good.

(Exodus 20:12.)

Thank You, Father,
that Your angels watch
over me. Any weapon
that is aimed at me
will be turned away.

(Isaiah 54:17; Psalm 91:11,12.)

Jesus, Your Word
keeps me doing things
that please You.

(Psalm 119:11.)

I do good things
because You're in
my heart.

(Matthew 12:35.)

Thank You, Jesus,
that because
I know You,
You give me
everything I need
to live a good life.

(2 Peter 1:3.)

Because I have
Your Word I know
the truth, and the
truth makes me free.

(John 8:32.)

No one can take
my joy from me, for
Jesus is my joy and
His joy makes me strong.

(John 16:22; Nehemiah 8:10.)

I have put Your Word in
my heart, and I know You
hear and answer my
prayer when I pray.

(Hebrews 11:1; Mark 11:24.)

Jesus inside of me is
bigger than the devil
who is in the world.

(1 John 4:4.)

Thank You, Father,
that You never leave me
alone or give up on me.

(Hebrews 13:5.)

I take the shield of faith
and I stop all the fiery
darts of the devil. I am
able to stand against
all of his mean tricks
with the Word of God.

(Ephesians 6:11.)

Jesus, when I say
Your name I can stand
against the devil and he
has to flee from me.

(James 4:7.)

Thank You, Jesus,
for giving me a chance
to do great things
for Your Kingdom.

(Revelation 3:8.)

Thank You, Jesus, that
You see and know what
makes me happy, and You
give me my heart's desire.

(Psalm 37:4.)

Your Word is in my heart
and protects me when
I'm asleep or awake.
Thank You, Father, for
always being with me.

(Proverbs 6:21,22.)

The sword of the spirit
is the Word of God.
When I say what God
says it brings me life
and makes me strong.

(Psalm 119:130; Ephesians 6:17.)

Prayer of Salvation

Father God,
I take Jesus as my Savior.
I love Him too.
Thank You for forgiving me
and making me new.
Amen.

Other Children's Books
From Harrison House Publishers

Prayers That Avail Much® for Kids,
Book 1

Prayers That Avail Much® for Kids,
Book 2

David and God's Covenant

Jesus Our Savior

Additional copies of this book are
available from your local bookstore.

Harrison House
Tulsa, Oklahoma 74153

Fast. Easy.
Convenient.

For the latest Harrison House product
information and author news, look no further
than your computer. All the details on our
powerful, life-changing products are just a
click away. New releases, E-mail subscriptions,
Podcasts, testimonies, monthly specials—find it
all in one place. Visit harrisonhouse.com today!

harrisonhouse

The Harrison House Vision

Proclaiming the truth and the power
Of the Gospel of Jesus Christ
With excellence;

Challenging Christians to
Live victoriously,
Grow spiritually,
Know God intimately.